Casualties of a Christmas Night Out

Malcolm Alexander

BookLeaf Publishing

Presentation by *BookLeaf Publishing*

Web: www.bookleafpub.com

E-mail: info@bookleafpub.com

ISBN: 9789357216333

First edition 2023

DEDICATION

To Rachel and Laura: this is entirely your fault.

PREFACE

When my friend suggested to me that this might be something I could do - a poem every day for 21 days, and a book at the end of it - I was initially horrified. However, the more I thought about it, the more it seemed like a good idea. In January 2022, I had set myself the challenge to write a poem - or just write something - every day that year so, surely, having the final few poems printed in a book was a great way to finish the year? And while a cynical observer might see it as a self-indulgent vanity project, who cares? After all, it is Christmas!

So here we are, 21 poems later, and what do we have? Tiny observations of the month, the season, the city, its people and its celebrations; my December.

Christmas in the City

Christmas comes in many colours and tones.
The lights will glow once the sun has set,
but for now they hang,
underwhelming passers-by,
parodies of decoration.
The frost will come,
dusting the world white and glittery,
but for now, the streets and spirits
are damp.
The music will play
and fill my heart full with
genuine festive cheer.
But for now the sounds
of Christmas are the mutterings
and murmurings of crowded streets
punctuated, here and there,
by fairground screams.

Winter Makes Fools of Us All

The mercury plummets today.
The pavements are thick with ice.
Winter pulls the ground from under me.

The sun glows weakly through the morning mist.
It warms nothing and lights so little.
Winter snaps at my fingers and toes.

Trains are absent; people are flummoxed.
Tickets are waved pointlessly at barriers and
railway staff.
Winter has wreaked its travel havoc.

It is -6C.
The man on the platform wears a hoodie,
unzipped
his ears redden in the late afternoon fog.
He paws at his phone with bare fingers,
and winter makes fools of us all.

Traindog

I find my seat,
collapse into it and prepare
for the arrival of
the conductor.

But suddenly
a white ear appears
from under the seat
across the aisle.
It is followed by
a black nose and two
brown eyes. He must be
freezing but he has on
a green, quilted Barbour
jacket which fends off
some of the bitter chill.

He looks up at me
as if to say,
Where's your ticket?

First of the Season

The first mince pie
of the season
winks at me from
its box.
We have searched
so long,
bizarrely, to no avail.

But it's Christmas, I cried
Where are all the mince pies?

But now it is mine,
well what do you think?
I shall eat you tomorrow
with a festive hot drink.
You'll be crumbly and sweet,
a real taste of the season,
All pastry and spice,
I need no other reason
to sit for a moment
munching sweet Christmas cheer,
my number one favourite
time of the year.

Evening

The sunset is dusted
across the bottom of
a deep blue sky;
the most immaculate blue.

The sunset glows
pale, almost watery
but clear and distinct
above the biting
winter skyline.
The cold claws at any exposed skin,
creeps under cuffs
and over collars,
fiercely reminding us that it is there.

But this,
this harsh evening,
is beautiful.

Snow Day

The snow leaps out
and grabs the day.
It surprises and delights
in equal measure.
The day has to slow down
and so it is late.
It shuffles in with
wet feet
and painfully cold hands.
It puts its damp gloves
onto the radiator,
then grumbles about the weather.

But it also smiles
and laughs
and enjoys this
surprise delivery of winter.

Casualties of the Christmas Night Out

On the pavement lies
the broken neck of a bottle,
green glass, cap still on;
a woolly, pom-pommed hat,
possibly abandoned, probably lost,
and my thoughts turn to
cold ears,exposed to the night air.
A pair of gloves, soaking
and sopping and twisted on the path.
Two hats, separate but
victims of the same mysterious fate:
abandoned but saved from the pavement,
angels on the railing trees.

Shadows of the night before;
remnants of a winter wonderland.

That's a Wrap

Paper and tape and string
and ribbon and tags and
ribbon and tape and paper
and tags and string.
I hunch over the tangle
of paraphernalia:
the paper is too big,
then too small;
the ribbon is too short
then far too long;
the tape will not hold
that corner,
then it pulls the coating off
that fold.
My back aches, my mind boggles.
But I am done
and surrounded by
the fruits of this
essential and infuriating Christmas labour.

Winter/ Not Wintry

Suddenly it is no longer cold.
Nearly twenty degrees difference
and a nation that had hunkered down
with extra layers and warm boots,
had turned the thermostat up and the fire on, had
stockpiled logs and dusted
off draught excluders,
was now faced with a day as mild as spring.
Coats and hats are now too thick,
rooms over-heated
and gloves barely needed.
Windows are thrown open
and quilts thrown off
At least until the real weather returns,
made of ice and frost and throwing
it's true winter weight around.

Decorations Of Red

Christmas bedsheets,
festive towels,
three glass bears,
two glittering owls.
Winter mugs,
a Santa plate,
a golden star,
a single ice skate.

A red plastic cuckoo clock,
from my gran's Christmas tree,
three soft felt stockings,
for him, you and me.
A seasonal tea cosy,
a snowman spoon stand,
my Santa Claus timer
I keep close at hand.
Twinkling lights
and winter spice candles,
a wreath for the door,
"Santa Stop" on the handle.
Our house decorations,
trinkets scattered around,
And enjoy! Cos in two weeks
it's all coming down.

The Solstice

The day begins
and then the sun rises.
We trundle on
but the light never really comes.
Yet, inside, where it is bright and welcoming,
bulbs burn and glow
keeping us safe and warm.
We are together and
despite the noise
it is lovely.

The sun sets,
the day draws
to a close and the
whoops and skirls
fade off out of the door
to their freedom and rest.
The day was brief
and despite giving us no real light,
it burned bright.

Face Hair

Ear hair, nose hair,
Beard bristles, hat fluff,
grow it long, trim it off,
too much, not enough.
Moustache strains a plate of soup,
Coffee froth, funny smell,
wipe my lip, brush my beard,
comb it too, looking swell.
Stray hairs, snip snip,
on and on, never done.
Sticking out, wax it down
Oh Christ, another one!
Start again, no-one knows
how to fix my
face-hair winter woes.

Memory Lane

I didn't mean it,
to drive down there.
I was making deliveries,
but on that road,
at this time of year,
without warning,
I found myself on Memory Lane.
In a van full of cakes -
though not a madeleine in sight -
this feeling rushed up
and surprised me,
tapped me on the shoulder
and enveloped me in the past.
It was street names and music,
and road junctions,
and it was warm and kind
and cheerful and sweet;
utterly familiar and
completely indescribable.

I sit for a moment
and as quickly as it arrived
the feeling was gone.

The Bauble

He held it so gently by its ribbon,
supporting it underneath
with his other hand.
He was so careful with it
because it contained so much:
memories, magical ideas, celebrations,
and, of course, love.
But as he sidled round the arm of the sofa,
negotiating the larger of the tree's branches,
it happened.
Perhaps his hands were too wee,
or the branch he chose too weak.
Perhaps he was just full of excitement,
of the season and the moment;
or there was simply too much at stake?
Whatever it was, as he stepped back,
the bauble fell from the branch
and for a split second the world stopped,
then it hit the floor
and smashed.
So much had been attached to this one fragile thing,
and it's demise left us, all three,
temporarily inconsolable.

Christmas in the Countryside

Here, the darkness is absolute and blinding.
The silence is true and deafening.
The sky is darker,
the stars so much more than just
silver dots in the black.
The sea lies absolutely still,
and stretches grey and unending before me.
Houses, in a nod to the neon of the city,
are decorated wildly and flicker and glow
illuminating the neighbourhood.

I lie awake and I yearn for the noise of the city,
for I can find no peace in this quiet.

On the Second Day of Christmas

One day on from The Big Day,
the three of us gather
in our living room
for our Christmas.
He is older and no longer
approaches the tree with
wide-eyed wonder,
astonished at how
Santa could have known;
he no longer tears off paper
and is frozen with excitement
at the discovery beneath.
But in place of this is a surprising patience,
and a time shared with us.
The paper is, of course, still torn but
his reaction now is a measured,
Joe Cool enthusiasm,
underplayed, grateful,
and filled with love.

The Christmas Bear

The tiny Christmas Queen of Bears sits
in her cracker crown
slowly posting chocolate Santas
into her mouth
and cackling about her brilliant ideas

Her face is part chocolate
and part giggle,
a grin smeared all over;
she drops the final silver wrapper
onto a paper plate
and runs off to pull
crackers with the world.

This is Christmas Too

This is Christmas too:
the rain hangs all around us,
uncertain whether to float off
or to soak us to the skin.
Potholes become puddles
on pavements and roads
and everyone is splashed
by everyone else who passes by.
Soggy trainers squelch on tourists' feet -
where on Earth
did they think they were coming?
Edinburgh's winter weather is erratic
and we must respect it
with appropriate footwear.
This is Christmas too:
we are between the big days,
and despite the rain
lights still twinkle
through the mist,
the streets are filled with people
and we trudge and splash
our way towards a new year.

The Close of Play

The end is in the air.
People gather to be together
to mark the occasion.

Once more it will draw to a close
but it will also be a marker
of the beginning

of a time when so much
has passed, that it is now
difficult to dwell on anything else.

People will cherish memories
of days when
favours were done and kindness shown.

They will hark back to those times
when they laughed, at and with,
and what they have learned in the process.

And they will puzzle and fret
over what to do now,
and how to do it after this end.

Time, Merry Gentlemen, Please.

It is time.
We had the conversation,
if you could even call it that,
and we both knew that
it was time.

The red, the glittery, the snow-flecked,
the cinnamon-spiced,
the mulled, the silvery, the piney,
the reindeer adorned,
the robin resplendent;
the snow-man'd and bestockinged,
candy striped, jingle belled,
Santa Claus covered clamjamphrie,
must leave us for another year;
Back into boxes and bags,
aloft and away.

Halls: undecked.

And finally...

We end as we began:
with drink and with music.
The day is now dark,
and this year is waning.
But the coming new year
promises light and brightness,
excitement and challenge;
and I welcome it with
open arms.

I sip my tea and
a song reminds me to
look to the stars;
for while they may
make us feel insignificant,
ultimately, they are magical,
and it is this
awe and wonder
that we must find in the
parks and paths,
cities and skies
in the unlikeliest places,
every single day.

www.ingramcontent.com/pod-product-compliance
Lightning Source LLC
Chambersburg PA
CBHW051719130826
49812CB00034B/1259
9789357216333